Java Quick Syntax Reference

Second Edition

Mikael Olsson

Apress®

Java Quick Syntax Reference

Mikael Olsson
Hammarland, Länsi-Suomi, Finland

ISBN-13 (pbk): 978-1-4842-3440-2   ISBN-13 (electronic): 978-1-4842-3441-9
https://doi.org/10.1007/978-1-4842-3441-9

Library of Congress Control Number: 2018932355

Copyright © 2018 by Mikael Olsson

Managing Director, Apress Media LLC: Welmoed Spahr
Acquisitions Editor: Steve Anglin
Development Editor: Matthew Moodie
Coordinating Editor: Mark Powers
Copyeditor: Corbin Collins

Cover designed by eStudioCalamar

Cover image designed by Freepik (www.freepik.com)

Distributed to the book trade worldwide by Springer Science+Business Media New York, 233 Spring Street, 6th Floor, New York, NY 10013. Phone 1-800-SPRINGER, fax (201) 348-4505, e-mail orders-ny@springer-sbm.com, or visit www.springeronline.com. Apress Media, LLC is a California LLC and the sole member (owner) is Springer Science + Business Media Finance Inc (SSBM Finance Inc). SSBM Finance Inc is a **Delaware** corporation.

For information on translations, please e-mail editorial@apress.com; for reprint, paperback, or audio rights, please email bookpermissions@springernature.com.

Apress titles may be purchased in bulk for academic, corporate, or promotional use. eBook versions and licenses are also available for most titles. For more information, reference our Print and eBook Bulk Sales web page at http://www.apress.com/bulk-sales.

Any source code or other supplementary material referenced by the author in this book is available to readers on GitHub via the book's product page, located at www.apress.com/9781484234402. For more detailed information, please visit www.apress.com/source-code.

Printed on acid-free paper

Table of Contents

About the Author

Mikael Olsson is a professional web entrepreneur, programmer, and author. He works for an R&D company in Finland where he specializes in software development. In his spare time he writes books and creates websites that summarize various fields of interest. The books he writes are focused on teaching their subject in the most efficient way possible, by explaining only what is relevant and practical without any unnecessary repetition or theory.

About the Technical Reviewer

Wallace Jackson has been writing for leading multimedia publications about his work in new media content development since the advent of *Multimedia Producer* magazine nearly two decades ago. He has authored a half dozen Android book titles for Apress, including four titles in the popular Pro Android series. Wallace received his undergraduate degree in business economics from the University of California at Los Angeles and a graduate degree in MIS design and implementation from the University of Southern California. He is currently the CEO of Mind Taffy Design, a new media content production and digital campaign design and development agency.

Introduction

Java is a high-level object-oriented programming language developed by
Sun Microsystems, which became part of Oracle Corporation in 2010. The
language is very similar to C++ but has been simplified to make it easier
to write bug-free code. Most notably, unlike C++, there are no pointers
in Java—instead, all memory allocation and deallocation is handled
automatically.

Despite simplifications like this, Java has considerably more
functionality than C++, due to its large class library. Java programs
also have high performance and can be made very secure, which
has contributed to making Java the most popular general-purpose
programming language in use today.

Another key feature of Java is that it is platform independent. This is
achieved by only compiling programs halfway, into platform-independent
instructions called *bytecode*. The bytecode is then interpreted, or run,
by the Java Virtual Machine (JVM). That means any system that has
this program and its accompanying libraries installed can run Java
applications.

To allow Java to be used in a variety of environments, there are four
different editions: Java ME, Java SE, Java EE, and Java FX. Each edition
contains a JVM and a set of class libraries. Java SE (Standard Edition)
provides the standard JVM along with the commonly used libraries for
building applications, in particular desktop applications. Java ME (Micro
Edition) is a small-footprint version of Java SE designed for running on
small devices such as mobile phones. Java EE (Enterprise Edition) is an
extended version of Java SE that includes libraries for building large-scale
web applications. The most recently added edition is JavaFX, a lightweight

version intended for building desktop and rich web applications. This edition includes a new library for making graphical user interfaces (GUIs), which is intended to replace the standard GUI library called Swing used in Java SE.

The Java language and class libraries have undergone major changes since their initial release in 1996. The naming conventions for the versions have gone through a few revisions as well. The major releases include JDK 1.0, JDK 1.1, J2SE 1.2, J2SE 1.3, J2SE 1.4, J2SE 5.0, Java SE 6, Java SE 7, Java SE 8, and Java SE 9, the current version as of writing.

After J2SE 1.4, the version number was changed from 1.5 to 5.0 for marketing reasons. As of J2SE 5.0, there is one version number for the product and another one used internally by the developers. J2SE 5.0 is the product name, whereas Java 1.5 is the developer version. Similarly, Java SE 9 is the product, and Java 1.9 the internal version number. For the sake of simplicity, the Java versions will be referred to as Java 1–9 in this book. Note that Java is designed to be backward-compatible. Therefore, the Virtual Machine for Java 9 can still run Java 1 applications.

CHAPTER 1

Hello World

Installing

Before you can program in Java you need to download and install a Java Development Kit (JDK), such as the Standard Edition (JDK SE) from Oracle's website.[1] Among other things, the JDK includes the Java compiler, the class libraries, and the virtual machine needed to run Java applications. Oracle's download page also has a link to obtain Netbeans[2] bundled with a JDK. Netbeans is an Integrated Development Environment (IDE) that will make development in Java much easier. Alternatively, another free IDE you can use is Eclipse.[3] If you don't want to use any IDE at all, a regular text editor will work just fine.

Creating a project

If you decide to use an IDE (recommended), you need to create a project, which will manage the Java source files and other resources. If you prefer not to use an IDE, you can create an empty file with the .java extension—for example, MyApp.java—and open it in your text editor of choice.

To create a project in Netbeans, click File ➤ New Project. In the dialog box select the Java Application project type under the Java category and click Next. In this dialog box set the project name to "MyProject" and

---

[1] www.oracle.com/technetwork/java/javase/downloads/index.html
[2] www.netbeans.apache.org
[3] http://www.eclipse.org

© Mikael Olsson 2018
M. Olsson, *Java Quick Syntax Reference*, https://doi.org/10.1007/978-1-4842-3441-9_1

the name of the main class to "myproject.MyApp". Change the project's location if you want and click Finish to generate the project. The project's only file, MyApp.java, will then open up, containing some default code. You can go ahead and remove all of that code so that you start with an empty source file.

Hello World

When you have your project and programming environment set up, the first application you will create is the Hello World program. This program will teach you how to compile and run Java applications, as well as how to output a string to a command window.

The first step in creating this program is to add a public class to your MyApp.java source file. The class must have the same name as the physical source file without the file extension—in this case, "MyApp". It's legal to have more than one class per file in Java, but only one public class is allowed, and that name must match the filename. Keep in mind that Java is case sensitive. The curly brackets following the class name delimit what belongs to the class and must be included. The brackets, along with their content, is referred to as a *code block*, or just a *block*:

```
public class MyApp {}
```

Java classes are organized into packages, which are similar to namespaces in other languages. A package statement needs to appear at the top of the file to designate which package a file belongs to. This name must match the directory the file is located in relative to the project's source directory, so in this case the package name is myproject:

```
package myproject;
public class MyApp {}
```

Next, add the main method inside the class. This is the starting point of the application and must always be included in the same form as is shown in the following code. The keywords themselves will be examined in later chapters:

```
package myproject;
public class MyApp {
  public static void main(String[] args) {}
}
```

The last step in completing the Hello World program is to output the text by calling the print method. This method is located inside the System class, and then another level down inside the out class. The method takes a single argument—the string to be printed—and it ends with a semicolon, as do all statements in Java:

```
package myproject;
public class MyApp {
  public static void main(String[] args) {
    System.out.print("Hello World");
  }
}
```

Note that the dot operator (.) is used to access members of a class. Similar to print, there's also the println method, which automatically adds a line break at the end of the printed string. The System class belongs to the java.lang package, which is always included in a Java project.

Code hints

If you're unsure of what a specific class contains, or what arguments a method takes, you can take advantage of code hints in some IDEs, such as Netbeans. The code hint window appears anytime you're typing code and there are multiple predetermined alternatives. You can also bring it up manually by pressing Ctrl+Spacebar. This is a powerful feature that gives you quick access to the class libraries and their members, along with descriptions.

CHAPTER 2

Compile and Run

Running from the IDE

With your Hello World program complete, you can compile and run it in one of two ways. The first method is by selecting Run from the menu bar of the IDE you're using. In Netbeans, the menu command is Run ➤ Run Project. The IDE will then compile and run the application, which displays the text "Hello World" in the output window of the IDE.

Running from a console window

The other way is to manually compile the program using a console window (C:\Windows\System32\cmd.exe). The most convenient way to do this is to first add the JDK bin directory to the PATH environment variable. In Windows, you do this using the SET PATH command and then by appending the path to your JDK installation's bin folder separated by a semicolon:

```
SET PATH=%PATH%;"C:\Program Files\JDK\bin"
```

By doing this, the console will be able to find the Java compiler from any folder for the duration of this console session. The PATH variable can also be permanently changed.[1] Next, navigate to the folder where the source file is located and run the compiler by typing *javac* followed by the complete filename:

```
javac MyApp.java
```

---

[1] www.java.com/en/download/help/path.xml

© Mikael Olsson 2018
M. Olsson, *Java Quick Syntax Reference*, https://doi.org/10.1007/978-1-4842-3441-9_2

The program will be compiled into a class file called MyApp.class. This class file contains bytecode instead of machine code, so to execute it you need to call the Java Virtual Machine by typing *java* followed by the filename:

```
java MyApp
```

Notice that the .java extension is used when compiling a file, but the .class extension is not used when running it.

Comments

Comments are used to insert notes into the source code and have no effect on the end program. Java has the standard C++ comment notation, with both single-line and multi-line comments:

```
// single-line comment

/* multi-line
   comment */
```

In addition to these, there is the Javadoc comment. This comment is used to generate documentation by using a utility included in the JDK bin folder, which is also called Javadoc:

```
/** javadoc
    comment */
```

CHAPTER 3

Variables

Variables are used for storing data in memory during program execution.

Data types

Depending on what data you need to store, there are several kinds of data types. Java has eight types built into the language, called *primitives*. The integer (whole number) types are byte, short, int, and long. The float and double types represent floating-point numbers (real numbers). The char type holds a Unicode character, and the boolean type contains either a true or false value. Except for these primitive types, every other type in Java is represented by a class, an interface, or an array.

Data Type	Size (Bits)	Description
byte	8	Signed integer
short	16	
int	32	
long	64	
float	32	Floating-point number
double	64	
char	16	Unicode character
boolean	1	Boolean value

© Mikael Olsson 2018
M. Olsson, *Java Quick Syntax Reference*, https://doi.org/10.1007/978-1-4842-3441-9_3

Declaring variables

To declare (create) a variable you start with the data type you want it to hold followed by a variable name. The name can be anything you want, but it's a good idea to give your variables names that are closely related to the values they will hold. The standard naming convention for variables is that the first word should be lowercase and any subsequent words initially capitalized:

```
int myInt;
```

Assigning variables

To give the variable a value you use the assignment operator (=) followed by the value. When a variable is initialized (assigned a value), it then becomes defined (declared and assigned):

```
myInt = 10;
```

The declaration and assignment can be combined into a single statement:

```
int myInt = 10;
```

If you need multiple variables of the same type, there is a shorthand way of declaring or defining them using the comma operator (,):

```
int myInt = 10, myInt2 = 20, myInt3;
```

Using variables

Once a variable has been defined, you can use it by simply referencing the variable's name—for example, to print it:

```
System.out.print(myInt);
```

Integer types

As shown earlier, there are four signed integer types you can use, depending on how large a number you need the variable to hold:

```
byte  myInt8  = 2;  // -128   to +127
short myInt16 = 1;  // -32768 to +32767
int   myInt32 = 0;  // -2^31  to +2^31-1
long  myInt64 = -1; // -2^63  to +2^63-1
```

In addition to standard decimal notation, integers can also be assigned by using octal or hexadecimal notation. As of Java 7, a binary notation is also available:

```
int myHex = 0xF;  // hexadecimal (base 16)
int myOct = 07;   // octal (base 8)
int myBin = 0b10; // binary (base 2)
```

Digits in a number can be separated by an underscore (_). This feature was introduced in Java 7 and is provided only to improve readability:

```
int bigNumber = 10_000_000;
```

Floating-point types

The floating-point types can store integers as well as floats. They can be assigned with either decimal or exponential notation:

```
double myDouble = 3.14;
double myDouble2 = 3e2; // 3*10^2 = 300
```

Note that constant floating-point numbers in Java are always kept internally as doubles. Therefore, if you try to assign a double to a float, you'll get an error because a double has a higher precision than a float. To assign it correctly you can append an *F* character to the constant, which says that the number is in fact a float:

```
float myFloat = 3.14;  // error
float myFloat = 3.14F; // ok
```

A more common and useful way to do that is by using an explicit cast. An *explicit cast* is performed by placing the desired data type in parentheses before the variable or constant that is to be converted. This will convert the value to the specified type—in this case, float—before the assignment occurs:

```
float myFloat = (float)3.14;
```

Char type

The char data type can contain a single Unicode character, delimited by single quotes:

```
char myChar = 'A';
```

Chars can also be assigned by using a special hexadecimal notation that gives access to all Unicode characters:

```
char myChar = '\u0000'; // \u0000 to \uFFFF
```

Boolean type

The boolean type can store a Boolean value, which is a value that can only be either true or false. These values are specified with the true and false keywords:

```
boolean myBool = false;
```

10

Variable scope

The *scope* of a variable refers to the code block within which it's possible to use that variable without qualification. For example, a *local variable* is a variable declared within a method. Such a variable will only be available within the method's code block, after it's been declared. Once the scope (code block) of the method ends, the local variable will be destroyed:

```
public static void main(String[] args)
{
  int localVar; // local variable
}
```

In addition to local variables, Java has field and parameter type variables, which later chapters will cover. But Java doesn't have global variables, as, for example, C++ does.

Anonymous block

You can restrict the scope of local variables using an *anonymous* (unnamed) code block. This construct is seldom used, because if a method is large enough to warrant the use of an anonymous block, a better choice is often to break up the code into separate methods:

```
public static void main(String[] args)
{
  // Anonymous code block
  {
    int localVar = 10;
  }
  // localVar is unavailable from here
}
```

11

CHAPTER 4

Operators

Operators are special symbols used to operate on values. They can be grouped into five types: arithmetic, assignment, comparison, logical, and bitwise operators.

Arithmetic operators

There are four basic arithmetic operators, as well as the modulus operator (%), which is used to obtain the division remainder:

```java
float x = 3+2; // 5 // addition
      x = 3-2; // 1 // subtraction
      x = 3*2; // 6 // multiplication
      x = 3/2; // 1 // division
      x = 3%2; // 1 // modulus (division remainder)
```

Note that the division sign gives an incorrect result. That's because it operates on two integer values and will therefore round the result and return an integer. To get the correct value, one of the numbers must be explicitly converted to a floating-point type:

```java
float x = (float)3/2; // 1.5
```

© Mikael Olsson 2018
M. Olsson, *Java Quick Syntax Reference*, https://doi.org/10.1007/978-1-4842-3441-9_4

Assignment operators

The second group is the assignment operators—most importantly, the assignment operator itself (=), which assigns a value to a variable.

Combined assignment operators

A common use of the assignment and arithmetic operators is to operate on a variable and then save the result back into that same variable. These operations can be shortened with the combined assignment operators:

```
int x = 0;
    x += 5; // x = x+5;
    x -= 5; // x = x-5;
    x *= 5; // x = x*5;
    x /= 5; // x = x/5;
    x %= 5; // x = x%5;
```

Increment and decrement operators

Another common operation is to increment or decrement a variable by one. This can be simplified with the increment (++) and decrement (--) operators:

```
++x; // x += 1
--x; // x -= 1
```

Both of these can be used either before or after a variable:

```
++x; // pre-increment
--x; // pre-decrement
x++; // post-increment
x--; // post-decrement
```

14

The result on the variable is the same whichever is used. The difference is that the post-operator returns the original value before it changes the variable, while the pre-operator changes the variable first and then returns the value:

```
x = 5; y = x++; // y=5, x=6
x = 5; y = ++x; // y=6, x=6
```

Comparison operators

The comparison operators compare two values and return either true or false. They're mainly used to specify *conditions*, which are expressions that evaluate to either true or false:

```
boolean x = (2==3); // false // equal to
        x = (2!=3); // true  // not equal to
        x = (2>3);  // false // greater than
        x = (2<3);  // true  // less than
        x = (2>=3); // false // greater than or equal to
        x = (2<=3); // true  // less than or equal to
```

Logical operators

The logical operators are often used together with the comparison operators. Logical *and* (&&) evaluates to true if both the left and right side are true, and logical *or* (||) is true if either the left or right side is true. For inverting a Boolean result, there is a logical *not* (!) operator. Note that for both logical *and* and logical *or*, the right-hand side won't be evaluated if the result is already determined by the left-hand side:

```
boolean x = (true && false); // false // logical and
        x = (true || false); // true  // logical or
        x = !(true);         // false // logical not
```

Bitwise operators

The bitwise operators can manipulate individual bits inside an integer. For example, the right shift operator (>>) moves all bits except the sign bit to the right, whereas zero-fill right shift (>>>) moves all bits right including the sign bit:

```
int x = 5 & 4; // 101 & 100 = 100 (4) // and
    x = 5 | 4; // 101 | 100 = 101 (5) // or
    x = 5 ^ 4; // 101 ^ 100 = 001 (1) // xor
    x = 4 << 1;// 100 << 1  =1000 (8) // left shift
    x = 4 >> 1;// 100 >> 1  =  10 (2) // right shift
    x = 4 >>>1;// 100 >>>1  =  10 (2) // zero-fill right shift
    x = ~4;     // ~00000100 = 11111011 (-5) // invert
```

These bitwise operators have shorthand assignment operators, just like the arithmetic operators:

```
int x = 5;
    x &= 5;   // "and" and assign
    x |= 5;   // or and assign
    x ^= 5;   // xor and assign
    x <<= 5;  // left shift and assign
    x >>= 5;  // right shift and assign
    x >>>= 5; // right shift and assign (move sign bit)
```

Operator precedence

In Java, expressions are normally evaluated from left to right. However, when an expression contains multiple operators, the precedence of those operators decides the order that they're evaluated in. The order of precedence is shown in the following table. This same order also applies to many other languages, such as C++ and C#.

Precedence	Operator	Precedence	Operator
1	++ -- ! ~	7	&
2	* / %	8	^
3	+ -	9		
4	<< >> >>>	10	&&
5	< <= > >=	11	||
6	== !=	12	= op=

For example, logical *and* (&&) binds weaker than relational operators, which in turn bind weaker than arithmetic operators:

```
x = 2+3 > 1*4 && 5/5 == 1; // true
```

To avoid having to learn the precedents of all operators and to clarify the intent, you can use parentheses to specify which part of the expression will be evaluated first. Parentheses have the highest precedence of all operators:

```
x = ( (2+3) > (1*4) ) && ( (5/5) == 1 ); // true
```

17

CHAPTER 5

String

The String class in Java is a data type that can hold string literals. *String* is a reference data type, as are all non-primitive data types. This means that the variable contains an address to an object in the memory, and not the object itself. A String object is created in the memory, and the address to the object is returned to the variable.

As seen in the following code, string literals are delimited by double-quotes. This is shorthand notation for the regular reference type initialization (creation) syntax, which uses the new keyword:

```java
String a = "Hello";
String b = new String(" World");
```

Combining strings

The plus sign is used to combine two strings. Known as the *concatenation* operator (+) in this context, it has an accompanying assignment operator (+=) that appends one string to another and creates a new string:

```java
String c = a+b; // Hello World
      a += b;  // Hello World
```

© Mikael Olsson 2018
M. Olsson, *Java Quick Syntax Reference*, https://doi.org/10.1007/978-1-4842-3441-9_5

Note that although a statement may be divided into multiple lines, a string must be on a single row unless it's split up using the concatenation operator:

```
String x
        = "Hello " +
          "World";
```

Escape characters

For adding new lines to the string itself, there is the escape character (\n). This backslash notation is used to write special characters, such as backslash and double-quote. Among the special characters is also a Unicode character notation for writing any character. All the escape characters can be seen in the following table.

Character	Meaning
\n	Newline
\t	Horizontal tab
\b	Backspace
\r	Carriage return
\uFFFF	Unicode character
	(4-digit hex number)
\f	Form feed
\'	Single quote
\"	Double-quote
\\	Backslash

String compare

The way to compare two strings is to use the equals method of the String class. If the equality operator (==) is used, the memory addresses will be compared instead:

```
boolean x = a.equals(b); // compares string
boolean y = (a == b);    // compares address
```

Bear in mind that all strings in Java are String objects. Therefore, it's possible to call methods directly on constant strings, just as it is on variables:

```
boolean z = "Hello".equals(a); // true
```

StringBuffer class

The String class has a large number of methods available, but it doesn't contain any methods for manipulating strings. That's because strings in Java are immutable. Once a String object has been created, the contents can't be changed unless the whole string is completely replaced. Because most strings are never modified, this was done on purpose to make the String class more efficient. For cases when you need a modifiable string, you can use the StringBuffer class, which is a mutable string object:

```
StringBuffer sb = new StringBuffer("Hello");
```

This class has several methods to manipulate strings, including append, delete and insert:

```
sb.append(" World");   // add to end of string
sb.delete(0, 5);       // remove 5 first characters
sb.insert(0, "Hello"); // insert string at beginning
```

21

You can convert a `StringBuffer` object back into a regular string with the `toString` method, which returns a string representation of the object. It exists for every class in Java, because it's defined by `Object`, which is inherited by all classes:

```
String s = sb.toString();
```

CHAPTER 6

Arrays

An *array* is a data structure used for storing a collection of values of a single type.

Array declaration

To declare an array, a set of square brackets is appended to the data type the array will contain, followed by the array's name. Arrays can be declared with any data type, and all of its elements must then be of that type:

```
int[] x;
```

Alternatively, the brackets may be placed after the array name. However, this form is discouraged. The brackets affect the type and should therefore appear next to the type:

```
int y[]; // discouraged form
```

Array allocation

The array is allocated with the new keyword, followed again by the data type and a set of square brackets containing the *length* of the array—the fixed number of elements the array can contain. Once the array is created, the elements will automatically be assigned to the default values for that data type:

```
int[] y = new int[3];
```

© Mikael Olsson 2018
M. Olsson, *Java Quick Syntax Reference*, https://doi.org/10.1007/978-1-4842-3441-9_6

Array assignment

To fill the array, elements can be referenced one at a time by placing the element's numerical index inside the square brackets and then assigning them values. Notice that the index starts with zero:

```
y[0] = 1;
y[1] = 2;
y[2] = 3;
```

Alternatively, the values can be assigned all at once using a curly bracket notation. The new keyword and data type may be optionally left out if the array is declared at the same time:

```
int[] x = new int[] {1,2,3};
int[] x = {1,2,3};
```

Once the array elements are initialized, they can be accessed by referencing the elements' indexes inside the square brackets:

```
System.out.print(x[0] + x[1] + x[2]); // "6"
```

Multi-dimensional arrays

Multi-dimensional arrays are declared, created, and initialized much like one-dimensional arrays, except that they have additional square brackets. They can have any number of dimensions, and for each dimension another set of square brackets is added:

```
String[][] x = {{"00","01"},{"10","11"}};
String[][] y = new String[2][2];

y[0][0] = "00";
y[0][1] = "01";
```

24

```
y[1][0] = "10";
y[1][1] = "11";

System.out.print(x[0][0] + x[1][1]); // "0011"
```

ArrayList class

Something important to keep in mind about arrays is that their length is fixed and there's no way to change their size. The size of an array can be retrieved through the length member of the array:

```
int x[] = new int[3];
int size = x.length; // 3
```

For cases when a resizable array is needed, the ArrayList class can be used, which is located in the java.util package. Items in the ArrayList are stored as the generic Object type. The ArrayList can therefore hold any data types, except for primitives:

```
// Create an Object ArrayList collection
java.util.ArrayList a = new java.util.ArrayList();
```

The ArrayList class has several useful methods to change the array, such as add, set, and remove:

```
a.add("Hi");        // add an element
a.set(0, "Hello"); // change first element
a.remove(0);        // remove first element
```

To retrieve an element from the ArrayList, you use the get method. The element then has to be explicitly cast back to its original type:

```
a.add("Hello World");
String s = (String)a.get(0); // Hello World
```

CHAPTER 7

Conditionals

Conditional statements are used to execute different code blocks based on different conditions.

If statement

The `if` statement will only execute if the condition inside the parentheses is evaluated to true. The condition can include any of the comparison and logical operators:

```java
if (x < 1) {
  System.out.println(x + " < 1");
}
```

To test for other conditions, the `if` statement can be extended by any number of `else if` clauses. Each additional condition will only be tested if all previous conditions are false:

```java
else if (x > 1) {
  System.out.println(x + " > 1");
}
```

The `if` statement can have one `else` clause at the end, which will execute if all previous conditions are false:

```java
else {
  System.out.println(x + " == 1");
}
```

© Mikael Olsson 2018
M. Olsson, *Java Quick Syntax Reference*, https://doi.org/10.1007/978-1-4842-3441-9_7

As for the curly brackets, they can be left out if only a single statement needs to be executed conditionally:

```
if (x < 1)
  System.out.println(x + " < 1");
else if (x > 1)
  System.out.println(x + " > 1");
else
  System.out.println(x + " == 1");
```

Switch statement

The switch statement checks for equality between an integer and a series of case labels. It then executes the matching case. The statement can contain any number of cases and may end with a default label for handling all other cases:

```
switch (y)
{
  case 0:  System.out.println(y + " is 0"); break;
  case 1:  System.out.println(y + " is 1"); break;
  default: System.out.println(y + " is something else");
}
```

Note that the statements after each case label aren't surrounded by curly brackets. Instead, the statements end with the break keyword. Without the break, the execution will fall through to the next case. This can be useful if several cases need to be evaluated in the same way.

Any integer data type can be used with a switch statement, including byte, short, int, and char. As of Java 7, the String type is also permitted:

```
String fruit = "apple";
switch (fruit)
```

```
{
  case "apple": System.out.println("apple"); break;
  default: System.out.println("not an apple"); break;
}
```

Ternary operator

In addition to the if and switch statements, there is the ternary operator
(?:). This operator can replace a single else if clause that assigns a value
to a specific variable. The operator takes three expressions. If the first one
is evaluated to true, then the second expression is returned, but if it's false,
the third one is evaluated and returned:

```
x = (x < 0.5) ? 0 : 1; // ternary operator (?:)
```

CHAPTER 8

Loops

There are four looping structures in Java. They're used to execute a specific code block multiple times. As with the conditional if statement, the curly brackets for the loops can be left out if there's only one statement in the code block.

While loop

The while loop runs through the code block only if the specified condition is true and will continue looping for as long as the condition remains true. The following loop will print out the numbers 0 to 9:

```java
int i = 0;
while (i < 10) {
  System.out.println(i++);
}
```

Note that the condition for the loop must evaluate to a boolean value. This condition is checked only at the start of each iteration (loop).

© Mikael Olsson 2018
M. Olsson, *Java Quick Syntax Reference*, https://doi.org/10.1007/978-1-4842-3441-9_8

Do while loop

The do while loop works the same way as the while loop, except that it checks the condition after the code block. It will therefore always run through the code block at least once:

```
int i = 0;
do {
  System.out.println(i++);
} while (i < 10);
```

For loop

The for loop is used to go through a code block a specific number of times. It uses three parameters. The first parameter initializes a counter and is always executed once, before the loop. The second parameter holds the condition for the loop and is checked before each iteration. The third parameter contains the increment of the counter and is executed at the end of each iteration:

```
for (int i = 0; i < 10; i++) {
  System.out.println(i);
}
```

Several variations of the for loop are possible. For instance, the first and third parameters can be split into several statements using the comma operator:

```
for (int k = 0, l = 10; k < 10; k++, l--) {
  System.out.println(k + l);
}
```

You also have the option of leaving out one or more of the parameters. For example, the third parameter can be moved into the body of the loop:

```
for (int k = 0, l = 10; k < 10;) {
  System.out.println(k + l); k++; l--;
}
```

For-each loop

The "for each" loop provides an easy way to iterate through arrays. On each iteration, the next element in the array is assigned to the specified variable, and the loop continues to execute until it has gone through the entire array:

```
int[] array = { 1,2,3 };
for (int element : array) {
  System.out.println(element);
}
```

Break and continue

There are two special keywords that can be used inside loops: break and continue. The break keyword ends the loop structure, and continue skips the rest of the current iteration and continues at the beginning of the next iteration:

```
break;    // end current loop
continue; // start next iteration
```

To break out of a loop above the current one, that loop must first be labeled by adding a name followed by a colon before it. With this label in place, it can now be used as an argument to the break statement, telling it which loop to break out of. This also works with the continue keyword in order to skip to the next iteration of the named loop. Note that the continue statement in this example is unreachable because the break statement prevents continue from executing:

```
myLoop: for (int i = 0, j = 0; i < 10; i++)
{
  while (++j < 10)
  {
    break myLoop;     // end for loop
    continue myLoop; // start next for iteration
  }
}
```

Labeled block

A *labeled* block, also called a *named* block, is created by placing a label before an anonymous code block. The break keyword can be used to break out of such a block, just as in labeled loops. This could be useful, for example, when performing a validation, where if one validation step fails the whole process must be aborted:

```
validation:
{
  if(true)
    break validation;
}
```

Labeled blocks can be useful for organizing a large method into sections. In most cases, splitting the method up is a better idea. But if the new method would require a lot of parameters, or if the method would only be used from a single location, then one or more labeled blocks may be preferable.

CHAPTER 9

Methods

Methods are reusable code blocks that only execute when called.

Defining methods

You can create a method by typing void followed by the method's name, a set of parentheses, and a code block. The void keyword means the method won't return a value. The naming convention for methods is the same as for variables—a descriptive name with the first word in lowercase and the first letter of any subsequent words capitalized:

```java
class MyApp
{
  void myPrint()
  {
    System.out.println("Hello");
  }
}
```

© Mikael Olsson 2018
M. Olsson, *Java Quick Syntax Reference*, https://doi.org/10.1007/978-1-4842-3441-9_9

Calling methods

The preceding method will simply print out a text message. To *invoke* (call) it from the main method, an instance of the MyApp class must be created first. The dot operator is then used after the instance's name in order to access its members, which include the myPrint method:

```
public static void main(String[] args)
{
  MyApp m = new MyApp();
  m.myPrint(); // "Hello"
}
```

Method parameters

The parentheses that follow the method name are used to pass arguments to the method. To do that, the corresponding parameters must first be added to the method declaration in the form of a comma-separated list:

```
void myPrint(String s)
{
  System.out.println(s);
}
```

A method can be defined to take any number of arguments, and they can have any data types. Just ensure that the method is called with the same types and number of arguments:

```
public static void main(String[] args)
{
  MyApp m = new MyApp();
  m.myPrint("Hello"); // "Hello"
}
```

To be precise, *parameters* appear in method definitions, whereas *arguments* appear in method calls. However, the two terms are sometimes used interchangeably.

Return statement

A method can return a value. The void keyword is then replaced with the data type the method will return, and the return keyword is added to the method body with an argument of the specified return type:

```
String getString()
{
  return "Hello";
}
```

return is a jump statement that causes the method to exit and return the specified value to the place where the method was called. For example, the preceding method can be passed as an argument to the getString method because the method evaluates to a string:

```
public static void main(String[] args)
{
  MyApp m = new MyApp();
  System.out.println( getString() ); // "Hello"
}
```

The return statement can also be used in void methods to exit before the end block is reached. When used in this context, no return value is specified:

```
void myPrint(String s)
{
  // Abort if string is empty
```

```
  if (s == "") { return; }

  System.out.println(s);
}
```

Method overloading

It's possible to declare multiple methods with the same name as long as the parameters vary in type or number. Called *method overloading,* this can, for example, be seen in the implementation of the System.out. println method. It's a powerful feature that allows a method to handle a variety of arguments without the programmer needing to be aware of using different methods:

```
void myPrint(String s)
{
  System.out.println(s);
}

void myPrint(int i)
{
  System.out.println(i);
}
```

Passing arguments

Java is different from many other languages in that all method parameters are passed by value. In fact, they can't be passed by reference. For value data types (primitive types), that means only a local copy of the variable is changed within the method, so the change won't affect the original variable. For reference data types (classes, interfaces, and arrays), it means only a copy of the memory address is passed to the method. Therefore, if the entire object is replaced, the change won't propagate back to the caller, but changes to the object will affect the original since the copy points to the same memory location:

```
public static void main(String[] args)
{
    int x = 0;                    // value data type
    m.set(x);                     // value is passed
    System.out.println(x);    // 0

    int[] y = {0};                // reference data type
    m.set(y);                     // address is passed
    System.out.println(y[0]); // 10
}

void set(int a) { a = 10; }
void set(int[] a) { a[0] = 10; }
```

CHAPTER 10

Class

A *class* is a template used to create objects. Classes are made up of members, the main two of which are fields and methods. *Fields* are variables that hold the state of the object, whereas *methods* define what the object can do—the so-called behaviors of the object:

```
class MyRectangle
{
  int x, y;
  int getArea() { return x * y; }
}
```

Object creation

To access a non-static class field or method from outside the defining class, an object of the class must first be created. That's done using the new keyword, which will create a new object in the system's memory:

```
public class MyApp
{
  public static void main(String[] args)
  {
    // Create an object of MyRectangle
    MyRectangle r = new MyRectangle();
  }
}
```

© Mikael Olsson 2018
M. Olsson, *Java Quick Syntax Reference*, https://doi.org/10.1007/978-1-4842-3441-9_10

An object is also called an *instance*. The object will contain its own set of fields, which can hold values that are different from those of other instances of the class.

Accessing object members

In addition to creating the object, the members of the class that are to be accessible beyond their package need to be declared as public in the class definition:

```
class MyRectangle
{
  public int x, y;
  public int getArea() { return x * y; }
}
```

The members of this object can now be reached by using the dot operator after the instance name:

```
public static void main(String[] args)
{
  MyRectangle r = new MyRectangle();
  r.x = 10;
  r.y = 5;
  int area = r.getArea(); // 50 (5*10)
}
```

Constructor

A class can have a *constructor*, a special kind of method used to instantiate (construct) the object. It always has the same name as the class and doesn't have a return type, since it implicitly returns a new instance of the class. To be accessible from another class not in its package, it needs to be declared with the public access modifier. When a new instance of the MyRectangle class is created using the new syntax, the constructor method is called, which in the following example sets the fields to the specified default values:

```
class MyRectangle
{
  int x, y;
  public MyRectangle() { x = 10; y = 20; }
}
```

The constructor can have a parameter list, like any other method. As shown in the following code, this can be used to make the fields' initial values depend on the parameters passed when the object is created:

```
class MyRectangle
{
  int x, y;
  public MyRectangle(int a, int b) { x = a; y = b; }
}

public class MyApp
{
  public static void main(String[] args)
  {
    MyRectangle r = new MyRectangle(20, 15);
  }
}
```

This keyword

Inside the constructor, as well as in other methods belonging to the object, a special keyword called this can be used. The this keyword is a reference to the current instance of the class. If, for example, the constructor's

43

parameters have the same names as the corresponding fields, then the fields could still be accessed by using the this keyword, even though they're overshadowed by the parameters:

```
class MyRectangle
{
  int x, y;
  public MyRectangle(int x, int y)
  {
    this.x = x;
    this.y = y;
  }
}
```

Constructor overloading

To support different parameter lists, the constructor can be overloaded. In the following example, if the class is instantiated without any parameters, the fields will be assigned the specified default values. With one parameter both fields will be set to the supplied value, and with two parameters each field will be assigned a separate value. Attempting to create an object with the wrong number of arguments or with incorrect data types will result in a compile-time error, just as with any other method:

```
class MyRectangle
{
  int x, y;
  public MyRectangle()          { x = 10; y = 20; }
  public MyRectangle(int a)      { x = a;  y = a;  }
  public MyRectangle(int a, int b) { x = a;  y = b;  }
}
```

Constructor chaining

You can also use the this keyword to call one constructor from another. Known as *constructor chaining*, this allows for greater code reuse. Note that the keyword appears as a method call, and that it must be on the first line in the constructor:

```
public MyRectangle()          { this(10, 20); }
public MyRectangle(int a)      { this(a, a);   }
public MyRectangle(int a, int b) { x = a; y = b; }
```

Initial field values

If there are fields in the class that need to be assigned default values, such as in the first constructor just shown, the fields can simply be assigned at the same time as they are declared. These initial values will be assigned before the constructor is called:

```
class MyRectangle
{
    int x = 10, y = 20;
}
```

Default constructor

It's possible to create a class even if no constructors are defined. That's because the compiler will then automatically create a default parameterless constructor:

```
class MyApp
{
    public static void main(String[] args)
    {
```

```
    // Default constructor used
    MyApp a = new MyApp();
  }
}
```

Null

The built-in constant `null` is used to represent an uninitialized object. It can only be assigned to objects and not to variables of primitive types. The equal-to operator (==) can be used to test whether an object is null:

```
String s = null;
// ...
if (s == null) s = new String();
```

Default values

The default value of an object is `null`. For primitive data types, the default values are as follows: numerical types become 0, a char has the Unicode character for zero (\0000), and a boolean is `false`. Default values will be automatically assigned by the compiler, but only for fields and not for local variables. However, explicitly specifying the default value for fields is considered good programming because it makes the code easier to understand. For local variables the default values aren't set by the compiler. Instead, the compiler forces the programmer to assign values to any local variables that are used so as to avoid problems associated with mistakenly using unassigned variables:

```
class MyApp
{
  int x; // field is assigned default value 0
```

```
int dummy() {
  int x; // local variable must be assigned if used
}
}
```

Garbage collector

The Java runtime environment has a garbage collector that periodically releases the memory used by objects when they're no longer needed. This frees the programmer from the often tedious and error-prone task of memory management. An object will be eligible for destruction when there are no more references to it. This occurs, for example, when the object goes out of scope. An object can also be explicitly dropped by setting its references to null:

```
class MyApp
{
  public static void main(String[] args)
  {
    MyApp a = new MyApp();

    // Make object available for garbage collection
    a = null;
  }
}
```

CHAPTER 11

Static

The static keyword is used to create fields and methods that can be accessed without having to make an instance of the class. Static (class) members only exist in one copy, which belongs to the class itself, whereas instance (non-static) members are created as new copies for each new object. That means static methods can't use instance members because these methods aren't part of an instance. On the other hand, instance methods can use both static and instance members:

```java
class MyCircle
{
  float r = 10;             // instance field
  static float pi = 3.14F; // static/class field

  // Instance method
  float getArea() { return newArea(r); }

  // Static/class method
  static float newArea(float a) { return pi*a*a; }
}
```

© Mikael Olsson 2018
M. Olsson, *Java Quick Syntax Reference*, https://doi.org/10.1007/978-1-4842-3441-9_11

Accessing static members

To access a static member from outside the class, the class name is used followed by the dot operator. This operator is the same as the one used to access instance members, but to reach them an object reference is required. Trying to access a static member by using an object reference (instead of the class name) will result in a warning since this makes it more difficult to see that a static member is being used:

```java
public static void main(String[] args)
{
  float f = MyCircle.pi;
  MyCircle c = new MyCircle();
  float g = c.r;
}
```

Static methods

The advantage of static members is that they can be used by other classes without having to create an instance of the class. Fields should therefore be declared static when only a single instance of the variable is needed. Methods should be declared static if they perform a generic function that's independent of any instance variables. A good example of this is the Math class which contains only static methods and fields:

```java
double pi = Math.PI;
```

Math is one of the classes that's included by default in every Java application, because it belongs to the java.lang package, which is always imported. This package contains classes fundamental to the Java language, such as String, Object, and System.

Static fields

Static fields have the advantage of persisting throughout the life of the application. That means they can be used, for example, to record the number of times a method has been called across all instances of the class. The initial value for a static field will only be set once, sometime before the class or field is ever used:

```
class MyCircle
{
  static void dummy() { count++; }
  static int count = 0;
}
```

Static initialization blocks

A *static initialization block* can be used if the initialization of static fields requires more than one line or some other logic. This block, in contrast to the constructor, will only be run once, at the same time as the static fields are initialized:

```
class MyClass
{
  static int[] array = new int[5];

  // Static initialization block
  static
  {
    int i = 0;
    for(int element : array)
      element = i++;
  }
}
```

Instance initialization blocks

An *initialization block* provides an alternative method for assigning instance fields. This block is placed on the class level, just like the static initialization block, but without the use of the static keyword. Any code placed between the brackets will be copied to the start of every constructor by the compiler:

```
class MyClass
{
  int[] array = new int[5];

  // Initialization block
  {
    int i = 0;
    for(int element : array) element = i++;
  }
}
```

A class can have multiple instance initialization and static initialization blocks.

CHAPTER 12

Inheritance

Inheritance allows a class to acquire the members of another class. In the following example, Apple inherits from Fruit. This is specified with the extends keyword. Fruit then becomes the superclass of Apple, which in turn becomes a subclass of Fruit. In addition to its own members, Apple gains all accessible members in Fruit, except for its constructors:

```java
// Superclass (parent class)
class Fruit
{
  public String flavor;
}

// Subclass (child class)
class Apple extends Fruit
{
  public String variety;
}
```

© Mikael Olsson 2018
M. Olsson, *Java Quick Syntax Reference*, https://doi.org/10.1007/978-1-4842-3441-9_12

Object

A class in Java may only inherit from one superclass, and if no class is specified it will implicitly inherit from Object. Therefore, Object is the root class of all classes:

```
// Same as class Fruit {}
class Fruit extends Object {}
```

Upcasting

Conceptually, a subclass is a specialization of the superclass. This means that Apple is a kind of Fruit, as well as an Object, and can therefore be used anywhere a Fruit or Object is expected. For example, if an instance of Apple is created, it can be *upcast* to Fruit because the subclass contains everything in the superclass:

```
Apple a = new Apple();
Fruit f = a;
```

The Apple is then seen as a Fruit, so only the Fruit members can be accessed:

```
f.flavor = "Sweet";
```

Downcasting

When the class is *downcast* back into an Apple, the fields that are specific to Apple will have been preserved. That's because the Fruit only contained the Apple—it didn't convert it. The downcast has to be made explicitly using the Java casting format because downcasting an actual Fruit object into an Apple isn't allowed:

```
Apple b = (Apple)f;
```

Instanceof operator

As a safety precaution, you can test to see whether an object can be cast to a specific class by using the instanceof operator. This operator returns true if the left side object can be cast into the right side type without causing an exception:

```
boolean b = (f instanceof Apple);
if (b == true)
  Apple c = (Apple)f;
```

CHAPTER 13

Overriding

A member in a subclass can redefine a member in its superclass. This is most often done to give instance methods new implementations.

Overriding members

In the following example, Rectangle's getArea method is overridden in Triangle by redeclaring it there with the same method signature. The signature includes the name, parameters, and return type of the method. However, the access level may be changed to allow for more access than the method being overridden:

```java
class Rectangle
{
  public int w = 10, h = 10;
  public int getArea() { return w * h; }
}

class Triangle extends Rectangle
{
  public int getArea() { return w * h / 2; }
}
```

Override annotation

To show that this override was intentional, the @Override annotation should be placed before the method. This annotation was added in Java 5 to prevent accidental overrides:

```
class Triangle extends Rectangle
{
  @Override public int getArea() {
    return w * h / 2;
  }
}
```

Invoking the getArea method from a Triangle instance will call Triangle's version of the method:

```
Triangle o = new Triangle();
o.getArea(); // (50) calls Triangle's version
```

If Triangle's instance is upcast into Rectangle, then Triangle's version of the method will still get called because Rectangle's version has been overridden:

```
Rectangle o = new Triangle();
o.getArea();  // (50) calls Triangle's version
```

Hiding members

This is only true for instance methods—not for class methods. If a class method called newArea is added to Rectangle and redefined in Triangle, then Triangle's version of the method will only hide Rectangle's implementation. Because of this, the @Override annotation isn't used:

```
class Rectangle
{
  public int w = 10, h = 10;
  public static int newArea(int a, int b) {
    return a * b;
  }
}

class Triangle extends Rectangle
{
  public static int newArea(int a, int b) {
    return a * b / 2;
  }
}
```

Calling newArea from Triangle's interface will, as expected, invoke Triangle's version, but calling the method from Rectangle's interface will invoke Rectangle's implementation:

```
Triangle o = new Triangle();
o.newArea(10,10); // (50) calls Triangle's version

Rectangle r = o;
r.newArea(10,10); // (100) calls Rectangle's version
```

Redefined instance methods will always be overridden in Java, and redefined class methods will always be hidden. There's no way to change this behavior, as can be done in C++ or C#, for example.

Preventing method inheritance

To prevent an instance method from being overridden in subclasses, you can declare it with the `final` modifier:

```
public final int getArea() { return w * h; }
```

Bear in mind that the order of the method modifiers isn't optional. The compiler will point out when the modifiers appear in the wrong order.

Accessing overridden methods

An overridden method can still be accessed from inside the subclass's instance methods using the `super` keyword. This keyword is a reference to the current instance of the superclass:

```
class Triangle extends Rectangle
{
  @Override public int getArea() {
    return super.getArea() / 2;
  }
}
```

Calling parent constructor

Another place where the `super` keyword can be used is on the first line of a constructor. There it can perform a method call that invokes the superclass's constructor:

```
public Triangle(int a, int b) { super(a,b); }
```

If the first line of a constructor isn't a call to another constructor, the Java compiler will automatically add a call to the superclass's parameterless constructor. That ensures that all ancestor classes are properly constructed:

```
public Triangle() { super(); }
```

CHAPTER 14

Packages and Import

Packages are used to avoid naming conflicts and to organize code files into different directories. So far in this book, the code file has been located at the root of the project's source directory and has therefore belonged to the so-called *default package*. In Java, the directory a file belongs to, relative to the project's source directory, corresponds to the package name.

To assign a code file to a package—for example, mypackage—it must be moved to a folder by that name, under the project directory. Furthermore, the file must specify which package it belongs to using the package keyword followed by the package name (and path). There may only be one package statement in each source file, and it must be the first line of code, except for any comments. Note that the naming convention for packages is all lowercase:

```
// This file belongs to mypackage
package mypackage;
```

Packages may be any number of directory levels deep, and the levels in the hierarchy are separated by dots. For example, if the mypackage folder containing the code file is placed in a project folder called sub, the package declaration would need to look like this:

```
package sub.mypackage;
```

© Mikael Olsson 2018
M. Olsson, *Java Quick Syntax Reference*, https://doi.org/10.1007/978-1-4842-3441-9_14

Accessing packages

To illustrate how to access package members, a file named MyClass.java is placed in the sub\mypackage folder under the project's source directory. The file contains a single public class called MyClass:

```
package sub.mypackage;
public class MyClass {}
```

MyClass can be accessed from another source file in one of two ways. The first way is to type the fully qualified name:

```
// Fully qualified class name
sub.mypackage.MyClass m;
```

The second option is to shorten the fully qualified name by including the class with the import keyword. An import statement must be located after the package declaration statement and before all other members in the code file. It has no other purpose than to free the programmer from having to type the fully qualified name:

```
import mypackage.sub.MyClass;
// ...
MyClass m;
```

In addition to importing a specific class, all types (classes or interfaces) inside of a package can be imported by using an asterisk (*). Note that this doesn't import any subpackages:

```
import java.util.*;
```

A third variation of the import statement is the static import, which imports all static members of a class. Once the static members are imported, they can be used without having to specify the class name:

```
import static java.lang.Math.*;
// ...
double pi = PI; // Math.PI
```

CHAPTER 15

Access Levels

There are four access levels available in Java: public, protected, private, and package-private. Package-private isn't explicitly declared using a keyword. Instead, it's the default access level for every member in Java:

```
public    int myPublic;    // unrestricted access
protected int myProtected;// package or subclass access
          int myPackage;   // package access
private   int myPrivate;   // class access
```

Private access

The most restrictive access level is private. Members with this level can only be used inside of the enclosing (containing) class:

```
package mypackage;
public class MyApp
{
  public    int myPublic;
  protected int myProtected;
          int myPackage;
  private   int myPrivate;
```

© Mikael Olsson 2018
M. Olsson, *Java Quick Syntax Reference*, https://doi.org/10.1007/978-1-4842-3441-9_15

```
  void test()
  {
    myPublic    = 0; // allowed
    myProtected = 0; // allowed
    myPackage   = 0; // allowed
    myPrivate   = 0; // allowed
  }
}
```

Package-private access

Package-private members can be accessed anywhere within the containing package, but not from another package:

```
package mypackage;
public class MyClass
{
  void test(MyApp m)
  {
    m.myPublic    = 0; // allowed
    m.myProtected = 0; // allowed
    m.myPackage   = 0; // allowed
    m.myPrivate   = 0; // inaccessible
  }
}
```

Protected access

Protected members are accessible within subclasses and within the containing package. Note that the meaning of *protected* in Java is different from other languages, such as C++ and C#, where protected members are only accessible from subclasses and the containing class:

```
package newpackage;
import mypackage.MyApp;

public class MyClass extends MyApp
{
  void test()
  {
    myPublic    = 0; // allowed
    myProtected = 0; // allowed
    myPackage   = 0; // inaccessible
    myPrivate   = 0; // inaccessible
  }
}
```

Public access

The public modifier gives unrestricted access from anywhere the member can be referenced:

```
package newpackage;
import mypackage.MyApp;

public class MyClass
{
  void test(MyApp m)
  {
```

```
   m.myPublic    = 0; // allowed
   m.myProtected = 0; // inaccessible
   m.myPackage   = 0; // inaccessible
   m.myPrivate   = 0; // inaccessible
  }
}
```

Top-level access

Members declared directly in the package—top-level members—may only choose between package-private and public access. For instance, a top-level class without an access modifier will default to package-private. Such a class will only be accessible within the containing package. In contrast, a top-level class explicitly declared as public can be reached from other packages as well:

```
// Accessible only from containing package
class PackagePrivateClass {}
```

```
// Accessible from any package
public class PublicClass {}
```

Nested class access

Java allows classes to be defined within other classes, and these are called *nested classes*. Such a class can have any one of the four access levels. If a class is inaccessible, it can't be instantiated or inherited:

```
public class MyClass
{
  // Only accessible within MyClass
  private class PrivateNestedClass {}
}
```

Access level guideline

As a guideline, when choosing an access level it's generally best to use the most restrictive level possible. That's because the more places a member can be accessed, the more places it can be accessed incorrectly, which makes the code harder to debug. Using restrictive access levels also makes it easier to modify the class without breaking the code for any other programmers using that class.

CHAPTER 16

Constants

A variable in Java can be made into a constant by adding the final keyword before the data type. This modifier means that the variable can't be reassigned once it's been set, and any attempts to do so will result in a compile-time error.

Local constants

A *local* constant must always be initialized at the same time as it's declared. The Java naming convention for constants is to use all uppercase letters and to separate words with underscores:

```
final double PI = 3.14;
```

Constant fields

Class and instance variables can also be declared as final:

```
class MyClass
{
  final double E = 2.72;
  static final double C = 3e8;
}
```

© Mikael Olsson 2018
M. Olsson, *Java Quick Syntax Reference*, https://doi.org/10.1007/978-1-4842-3441-9_16

In contrast to local constants, *constant* fields don't have to be assigned at declaration. A constant instance field can optionally be assigned in a constructor, and a constant static field may be assigned by using a static initialization block. These alternative assignments can be useful if the constant's value needs to be calculated and doesn't fit on a single code line:

```
class MyClass
{
  final double E;
  static final double C;

  public MyClass() { E = 2.72; }
  static { C = 3e8; }
}
```

Constant method parameters

Another place where the final modifier may be applied is to method parameters to make them unchangeable. Doing so provides a signal to other developers that the method won't modify the argument passed to it:

```
void f(final String A) {}
```

Compile-time and runtime constants

Like most other languages, Java has both compile-time and runtime constants. However, only class constants can be compile-time constants in Java, and only if their value is known at compilation. All other uses of final will create runtime constants. With compile-time constants, the compiler will replace the constant name everywhere in the code with its value. These are therefore faster than runtime constants, which aren't set until the program is run. Runtime constants, though, can be assigned dynamic values that can change from one program run to the next:

```
class MyClass
{
  // Compile-time constant (static and known at compile-time)
  final static double C = 3e8;

  // Run-time constant (not static)
  final double E = 2.72;

  // Run-time constant (not known at compile-time)
  final static int RND = (new
  java.util.Random()).nextInt();
}
```

Constant guideline

In general, it's a good idea to always declare variables as final, and constant fields as static final, if they don't need to be reassigned. That ensures that the fields and variables won't be changed anywhere in the program by mistake, which in turn helps prevent bugs.

CHAPTER 17

Interface

The interface type is used to specify methods that classes implementing the interface must define. These methods are created with the interface keyword followed by a name and a code block. Their naming convention is the same as for classes: the first letter of each word is capitalized:

```
interface MyInterface {}
```

When an interface isn't nested inside another type, its access level can be either package-private or public, just like any other top-level member.

Interface members

The code block for an interface can, first of all, contain signatures for instance methods. These methods don't have any implementations. Instead, their bodies are replaced by semicolons. Interface members have public access by default, so this modifier can be left out:

```
interface MyInterface {
  int myMethod(); // method signature
}
```

The second member that an interface can contain is constants. Any field created in an interface will be implicitly declared as static final, so these modifiers can also be left out:

```
interface MyInterface {
  int c = 10; // constant
}
```

In addition to method signatures and constants, an interface can also contain nested containing types, such as classes or other interfaces:

```
interface MyInterface
{
  // Types
  class Class {}
  interface Interface {}
  enum Enum {}
}
```

Interface example

The following example shows an interface called Comparable, which has a single method named compare:

```
interface Comparable
{
  int compare(Object o);
}
```

The following class implements this interface using the implements keyword after the class name. By convention, the implements clause is placed after the extends clause if the class has one. Note that although a class can only inherit from one superclass, it may implement any number of interfaces by specifying them in a comma-separated list:

```
class Circle implements Comparable
{
  public int r;
}
```

Because Circle implements Comparable, it must define the compare method. For this class, the method will return the difference between the circle radiuses. The implemented method must be public and must have the same signature as the method defined in the interface:

```
class Circle implements Comparable
{
  public int r;

  public int compare(Object o) {
    return r - ( (Circle)o ).r;
  }
}
```

Functionality interface

Comparable demonstrates the first use of interfaces, which is to define a specific functionality that classes can share. It makes it possible to use the interface members without having to know the actual type of a class. To illustrate, the next example shows a simple method that takes two Comparable objects and returns the largest one. This method will work for any class that implements the Comparable interface because the method only uses the functionality exposed through that interface:

```
public static Object largest(Comparable a, Comparable b)
{
  return (a.compare(b) > 0) ? a : b;
}
```

Class interface

A second way to use an interface is to provide an actual interface for a class, through which the class can be used. The following example defines an interface for MyClass called MyInterface. This interface only includes the functionality that programmers using MyClass may need:

```
interface MyInterface
{
  void exposed();
}

class MyClass implements MyInterface
{
  public void exposed() {}
  public void hidden() {}
}
```

The interface type is then used to hold the implementing class so the class is only seen through this interface:

```
public static void main(String[] args)
{
  MyInterface i = new MyClass();
}
```

   This abstraction provides two benefits. First, it makes it easier for other programmers to use the class because they now only have access to the methods that are relevant. Second, it makes the class more flexible because its implementation can change, without being noticeable by other programmers using the class, as long as the interface is followed.

Interface classes

As mentioned, an interface can contain nested types, such as classes. In contrast to methods, these types are implemented inside the interface. This can, for example, be used to provide a class that contains static methods useful for implementing classes. These nested types are only visible to classes implementing the interface, and not to objects of those classes:

```
interface MyInterface
{
  class HelperClass {
    public static void helperMethod() {}
  }
}
```

Interface methods

Java 8 added the ability to define default methods in interfaces. Such a method is specified using the default keyword and can then include an implementation inside the interface:

```
interface MyInterface
{
  default void defaultMethod() {
```

```
    System.out.println("default");
  }
}
```

A default method will be used unless it's overridden by an implementing class. This provides a backward-compatible way to add new methods to an interface without breaking existing classes that use the interface:

```
class MyClass implements MyInterface
{
  public static void main(String[] args) {
    MyInterface i = new MyClass();
    i.defaultMethod(); // "default"
  }
}
```

Another feature introduced in Java 8 was static interface methods. Similar to static class methods, these methods belong to the interface and can only be called from an interface context:

```
interface MyInterface
{
  static void staticMethod() {
    System.out.println("static");
  }
}

class MyClass
{
  public static void main(String[] args) {
    MyInterface.staticMethod(); // "static"
  }
}
```

As of Java 9, static methods can have private access. This enables lengthy default methods to be split across private methods, which allows for less code duplication:

```java
interface MyInterface
{
  private static String getString() {
    return "string";
  }

  default void printString() {
    System.out.println(getString());
  }
}
```

CHAPTER 18

Abstract

An *abstract* class provides a partial implementation that other classes can build upon. When a class is declared `abstract`, it means it can contain incomplete methods that must be implemented in subclasses, in addition to normal class members. These methods are left unimplemented and only specify their signatures, while their bodies are replaced by semicolons:

```java
abstract class Shape
{
  public int x = 100, y = 100;
  public abstract int getArea();
}
```

Abstract class example

If a class called `Rectangle` inherits from the abstract class `Shape`, `Rectangle` is then forced to override the abstract `getArea` method. The only exception is if `Rectangle` is also declared `abstract`, in which case it doesn't have to implement any abstract methods:

```java
class Rectangle extends Shape
{
  @Override public int getArea() {
    return x * y;
  }
}
```

© Mikael Olsson 2018
M. Olsson, *Java Quick Syntax Reference*, https://doi.org/10.1007/978-1-4842-3441-9_18

An abstract class can't be instantiated, but it can be used to hold instances of its subclasses:

```
Shape s = new Rectangle();
```

Even though an abstract class can't be instantiated, it may have constructors, which can be called from the subclass's constructors using the super keyword:

```
abstract class Shape
{
  public int x = 100, y = 100;
  public Shape(int a, int b) {
    x = a;
    y = b;
  }
}

class Rectangle extends Shape
{
  public Rectangle(int a, int b) {
    super(a,b);
  }
}
```

Abstract classes and interfaces

Abstract classes are similar to interfaces in many ways. They can both define method signatures that subclasses must implement, and neither one of them can be instantiated. One key difference is that an abstract class can contain any abstract or non-abstract member, whereas an interface is limited to abstract members, nested types, and static constants, as well as static methods and default methods as of Java 8. Another difference is that a class can implement any number of interfaces but only inherit from one class, abstract or not.

An interface is either used to define a specific functionality that a class can have or to provide an interface for other developers using a class. In contrast, an abstract class is used to provide a partial class implementation, leaving it up to subclasses to complete it. This is useful when subclasses have some functionality in common but also have some functionality that must be implemented differently for each subclass.

CHAPTER 19

Enum

An *enumeration*, or *enum*, is a type that consists of a fixed list of named constants. To create one, the enum keyword is used followed by a name and a code block containing a comma-separated list of constant elements. The access level for an enum is the same as for a class. Package-private by default, but it can also be set to public if it's declared in a file of the same name. As with classes, an enum can be contained within a class, where it can then be set to any access level:

```
enum Speed
{
  STOP, SLOW, NORMAL, FAST
}
```

An object of the enum type just shown can hold any one of the four defined constants. The enum constants are accessed as if they were static fields of a class:

```
Speed s = Speed.SLOW;
```

The switch statement provides a good example of when an enumeration can be useful. Compared to using ordinary constants, an enum has the advantage of allowing the programmer to clearly specify what constant values are allowed. This provides compile-time type safety.

© Mikael Olsson 2018
M. Olsson, *Java Quick Syntax Reference*, https://doi.org/10.1007/978-1-4842-3441-9_19

Note that when using an enum in a `switch` statement, the case labels aren't qualified with the name of the enum:

```
switch(s)
{
  case SLOW: break;
}
```

Enum class

In Java, the enum type is more powerful than its counterparts in other languages, such as C++ or C#. Essentially a special kind of class, it can include anything a class can include. To add a class member, the list of constants must be terminated with a semicolon, and the member must be declared after the constants. In the following example, an integer is added to the enum, which will hold the actual speed that the elements represent:

```
enum Speed
{
  STOP, SLOW, NORMAL, FAST;
  public int speed;
}
```

To set this field, a constructor needs to be added as well. A constructor in an enum must have either private or package-private access and isn't called in the same way as for a regular class. Instead, the parameters to the constructor are given after the constant elements, as seen in the next example. If a Speed enum object is assigned the constant SLOW, then the argument 5 will be passed to the constructor for that enum instance:

```
enum Speed
{
  STOP(0), SLOW(5), NORMAL(10), FAST(20);
  public int speed;
```

```
    Speed(int s) { speed = s; }
}
```

Another difference that enum types have when compared to regular classes, is that they implicitly extend from the java.lang.Enum class. In addition to the members inherited from this class, the compiler will also automatically add two static methods to the enumeration, namely values and valueof. The values method returns an array of the constant elements declared in the enum, and valueof returns the enum constant of the specified enum name:

```
Speed[] a = Speed.values();
Speed s = Speed.valueOf(a[0].toString()); // Speed.STOP
```

CHAPTER 20

Exception Handling

Exception handling allows programmers to deal with unexpected situations that may occur in their programs. For example, the FileReader class in the java.io package is used to open a file. Creating an instance of this class will cause Netbeans to give a reminder that the class's constructor may throw a FileNotFoundException. Attempting to run the program will also cause the compiler to point this out:

```java
import java.io.*;
public class MyClass
{
  public static void main(String[] args)
  {
    // Compile-time error
    FileReader file = new FileReader("missing.txt");
  }
}
```

Try-catch

To handle this compile-time error the exception must be caught by using a try-catch statement. This statement consists of a try block containing the code that may cause the exceptions and one or more catch clauses. If the try block executes successfully, the program will continue running after

© Mikael Olsson 2018
M. Olsson, *Java Quick Syntax Reference*, https://doi.org/10.1007/978-1-4842-3441-9_20

the try-catch statement, but if an exception occurs, execution will then be passed to the first catch block able to handle that exception type:

```
try {
  FileReader file = new FileReader("missing.txt");
}
catch(FileNotFoundException e) {}
```

Catch block

In the preceding example, the catch block is only set to handle the FileNotFoundException. If the code in the try block could throw more kinds of exceptions, and all of them should be handled in the same way, a more general exception can be caught instead, such as the Exception class itself from which all exceptions derive. This catch clause would then be able to handle all the exceptions that inherit from this class, including the FileNotFoundException. Bear in mind that a more general exception needs to be caught after a more specific exception. The catch clause must always define an exception object. This object can be used to obtain more information about the exception, such as a description of the exception using the getMessage method:

```
catch(FileNotFoundException e) {
  System.out.print(e.getMessage());
}
catch(Exception e) {
  System.out.print(e.getMessage());
}
```

As of Java 7, multiple exceptions of different types can be caught using a single catch block. This helps avoid code duplication, without having to catch an overly general exception type, in cases when multiple exceptions are to be handled in the same way. Each exception is separated with a vertical bar (|) in the catch clause:

```
catch(IOException | SQLException e) {
  // Handle exception
}
```

Finally block

As the last clause in a try-catch statement, a finally block can be added. This block is used to clean up resources allocated in the try block and will always execute whether or not there's an exception. In this example, the file opened in the try block should be closed, but only if it was successfully opened. To be able to access the FileReader object from the finally clause, it must be declared outside of the try block. Additionally, because the close method can also throw an exception, the method needs to be surrounded with another try-catch block. Keep in mind that if you forget to close a resource object, Java's garbage collector will eventually close the resource for you, but closing it yourself is good programming practice:

```
FileReader file = null;
try {
  file = new FileReader("missing.txt");
}
catch(FileNotFoundException e) {
  System.out.print(e.getMessage());
}
finally {
  if (file != null) {
    try { file.close(); }
    catch(IOException e) {}
  }
}
```

Java 7 added the ability to automatically close resource objects by defining the resource object in parentheses after the try keyword. For this to work, the resource must implement the java.lang.AutoClosable interface. This interface consists of only the close method, which is called automatically in an implicit finally statement. The preceding example can now be simplified as follows:

```
try(FileReader file = new FileReader("missing.txt")) {
  // Read file
}
catch(FileNotFoundException e) {
  // Handle exception
}
```

More than one resource object can be included for automatic closing. As of Java 9, objects declared outside of the parentheses can also be referenced, provided they're final or effectively final:

```
// Final resource
final FileReader file1 = new FileReader("file1.txt");

// Effectively final resource
FileReader file2 = new FileReader("file2.txt");

try(file1; file2) {
  // Read files
}
catch(FileNotFoundException e) {
  // Handle exception
}
```

Throwing exceptions

When a situation occurs that a method can't recover from, it can generate its own exception to signal to the caller that the method has failed. It does that using the throw keyword followed by a new instance of a Throwable type:

```
static void MakeException()
{
  throw new Throwable("My Throwable");
}
```

Checked and unchecked exceptions

Exceptions in Java are grouped into two categories—checked and unchecked—depending on whether or not they need to be specified. A method that throws a checked exception—for example, IOException—will not compile unless it's specified using a throws clause after the method's parameter list and the calling method catches the exception. Unchecked exceptions, on the other hand, such as the ArithmeticException, do not have to be caught or specified. Note that to specify multiple exceptions, the exception types are separated by a comma:

```
static void MakeException()
throws IOException, ArithmeticException
{
  // ...
  throw new IOException("My IO exception");
  // ...
  throw new ArithmeticException("Division by zero");
}
```

Exception hierarchy

Exceptions, like most everything else in Java, are classes that exist in a hierarchy. At the root of this hierarchy (below `Object`) is the `Throwable` class, and all descendants of this class can be both thrown and caught. Inheriting from `Throwable` are the `Error` and `Exception` classes. Classes descending from `Error` are used to indicate non-recoverable exceptions, such as the `OutOfMemoryError`. These are unchecked because once they've occurred it's unlikely that the programmer can do anything about them even if they're caught.

Descending from `Exception` are the `RuntimeExceptions`, which are also unchecked. These are exceptions that can occur in almost any code, and it would therefore be cumbersome to catch and specify them. For example, a division by zero will throw an `ArithmeticException`, but surrounding every division operation with a `try-catch` would be bothersome. There's also some overhead associated with checking for exceptions, and the cost of checking for these exceptions outweighs the benefit of catching them. The other `Exception` descendants, those that don't inherit from `RuntimeExceptions`, are all checked. These are exceptions that can be recovered from and that must be both caught and specified.

CHAPTER 21

Boxing and Unboxing

Placing a primitive variable in an object is known as *boxing*. Boxing allows the primitive to be used where objects are required. For this purpose, Java provides wrapper classes to implement boxing for each primitive type—namely, Byte, Short, Integer, Long, Float, Double, Character, and Boolean. An Integer object, for example, can hold a variable of the type int:

```
int iPrimitive = 5;
Integer iWrapper = new Integer(iPrimitive); // boxing
```

The opposite of boxing is, naturally, *unboxing*, which converts the object type back into its primitive type:

```
iPrimitive = iWrapper.intValue(); // unboxing
```

The wrapper classes belong to the java.lang package, which is always imported. When using wrapper objects, keep in mind that the equal to operator (==) checks whether both references refer to the same object, whereas the equals method is used to compare the values that the objects represent:

```
Integer x = new Integer(1000);
Integer y = new Integer(1000);
boolean b = (x == y);    // false
        b = x.equals(y); // true
```

© Mikael Olsson 2018
M. Olsson, *Java Quick Syntax Reference*, https://doi.org/10.1007/978-1-4842-3441-9_21

Autoboxing and autounboxing

Java 5 introduced *autoboxing* and *autounboxing*. These features allow for automatic conversion between primitives and their wrapper objects:

```
Integer iWrapper = iPrimitive; // autoboxing
iPrimitive = iWrapper;         // autounboxing
```

Note that this is only syntactic sugar designed to make the code easier to read. The compiler will add the necessary code to box and unbox the primitives for you, using the `valueOf` and `intValue` methods:

```
Integer iWrapper = Integer.valueOf(iPrimitive);
iPrimitive = iWrapper.intValue()
```

Primitive and wrapper guideline

Primitive types should be used when there's no need for objects. That's because primitives are generally faster and more memory efficient than objects. Conversely, wrappers are useful when numerical values are needed but objects are required. For example, to store numerical values in a collection class, such as `ArrayList`, the wrapper classes are needed:

```
java.util.ArrayList a = new java.util.ArrayList();
a.add(Integer.valueOf(5)); // boxing
a.add(10);                 // autoboxing
```

Bear in mind that conversions between primitives and wrapper objects should be kept low if speed is important. There's an inherit performance penalty associated with any boxing and unboxing operation.

CHAPTER 22

Generics

Generics refers to the use of type parameters, which provide a way to define methods, classes, and interfaces that can operate with different data types. The benefits of generics are that they provide compile-time type safety and they eliminate the need for most type conversions.

Generic classes

Generic classes allow class members to use type parameters. Such a class is defined by adding a type parameter section after the class name, which contains a type parameter enclosed between angle brackets. The naming convention for type parameters is that they should consist of a single uppercase letter. Typically, the letter T for *type* is used. The following example defines a generic container class that can hold a single element of the generic type:

```
// Generic container class
class MyBox<T> { public T box; }
```

When an object of this generic class is instantiated, the type parameter must be replaced with an actual data type, such as `Integer`:

```
MyBox<Integer> iBox = new MyBox<Integer>();
```

© Mikael Olsson 2018
M. Olsson, *Java Quick Syntax Reference*, https://doi.org/10.1007/978-1-4842-3441-9_22

Alternatively, as of Java 7, a generic class can be instantiated with an empty set of type parameters. This type of instantiation is possible as long as the compiler can infer (determine) the type parameters from the context:

```
MyBox<Integer> iBox = new MyBox<>();
```

When an instance of MyBox is created, each type parameter in the class definition is replaced with the passed-in type argument. The object therefore behaves as a regular object, with a single field of the Integer type:

```
iBox.box = 5;
Integer i = iBox.box;
```

Notice that no casting is required when the stored value is set or retrieved from the box field. Furthermore, if the generic field is mistakenly assigned to or set to an incompatible type, the compiler will point that out:

```
iBox.box = "Hello World"; // compile-time error
String s = iBox.box;      // compile-time error
```

Generic methods

A method can be made generic by declaring it with a type parameter section before the method's return type. The type parameter can be used like any other type inside of the method. You can also use it for the method's return type, in the throws clause and for its parameter types. The next example shows a generic class method that accepts a generic array parameter, the content of which is printed out:

```
class MyClass
{
  public static <T> void printArray(T[] array)
  {
```

```
    for (T element : array)
      System.out.println(element);
  }
}
```

The preceding shown class isn't generic. Methods can be declared as generic, independently of whether or not the enclosing class or interface is generic. The same is true for constructors.

Calling generic methods

A generic method is typically invoked just as a regular (non-generic) method, without specifying the type argument:

```
Integer[] iArray = { 1, 2, 3 };
MyClass.printArray(iArray);
```

In most cases, the Java compiler can infer the type argument of a generic method call, so it doesn't have to be included. But if that's not the case, then the type argument will need to be explicitly specified:

```
MyClass.<Integer>printArray(iArray);
```

Generic interfaces

Interfaces that are declared with type parameters become generic interfaces. Generic interfaces have the same two purposes as regular interfaces: they're either created to expose members of a class that will be used by other classes, or to force a class to implement a specific functionality. When a generic interface is implemented, the type argument must be specified. The generic interface can be implemented by both generic and non-generic classes:

```
// Generic functionality interface
interface IGenericCollection<T>
{
  public void store(T t);
}

// Non-generic class implementing generic interface
class Box implements IGenericCollection<Integer>
{
  public Integer myBox;
  public void store(Integer i) { myBox = i; }
}

// Generic class implementing generic interface
class GenericBox<T> implements IGenericCollection<T>
{
  public T myBox;
  public void store(T t) { myBox = t; }
}
```

Generic type parameters

The passed-in type argument for a generic can either be a class type, interface type, or another type parameter, but it can't be a primitive type. Generics can have more than one type parameter defined, by adding more of them between the angle brackets in a comma-separated list. Bear in mind that each parameter within the brackets must be unique:

```
class MyClass<T, U> {}
```

If a generic has multiple type parameters defined, the same number of type arguments need to be specified when the generic is used:

```
MyClass<Integer, Float> m = new MyClass<Integer, Float>();
```

Generic variable usages

Generics are only a compile-time construct in Java. After the compiler has checked that the types used with generic variables are correct, it will then erase all type-parameter and argument information from the generic code and insert the appropriate casts instead. That means generics don't provide any performance benefits over non-generic code, because of removed runtime casts, as they do in, for example, C#. It also means generic types can't be used for anything that requires runtime information—such as creating new instances of generic types or using the instanceof operator with type parameters. Operations that are allowed include declaring variables of the generic type, assigning null to generic variables, and calling Object methods:

```
class MyClass<T>
{
  public void myMethod(Object o)
  {
    T t1;                              // allowed
    t1 = null;                         // allowed
    System.out.print(t1.toString());   // allowed
    if (o instanceof T) {}             // invalid
    T t2 = new T();                    // invalid
  }
}
```

The process of removing type information from generic code is known as *type erasure*. For example, MyBox<Integer> would be reduced to MyBox, which is called the *raw type*. This step is performed in order to maintain backward-compatibility with code written before generics became part of the language in Java 5.

Bounded type parameters

It's possible to apply compile-time enforced restrictions on the kinds of type parameters that a generic may be used with. These restrictions, called *bounds*, are specified within the type parameter section using the extends keyword. Type parameters can be bounded by either superclass or interface. For example, the following class B may only be instantiated with a type argument that's either of the type A or has that class as a superclass:

```
// T must be or inherit from A
class B<T extends A> {}
class A {}
```

The next example specifies an interface as the bound. This will restrict the type parameter to only those types that implement the specified interface or are of the interface type itself:

```
// T must be or implement interface I
class C<T extends I> {}
interface I {}
```

Multiple bounds can be applied to a type parameter by specifying them in a list separated by ampersands:

```
class D<T extends A & I> {}
```

The ampersand acts as the separator instead of a comma because comma is already used for separating type parameters:

```
class E<T extends A & I, U extends A & I> {}
```

Aside from restricting the use of a generic to only certain parameter types, another reason for applying bounds is to increase the number of permitted method calls supported by the bounded type. An unbounded type may only call the Object methods. However, by applying a superclass or interface bound, the accessible members of that type will also become available:

```
class Fruit
{
  public String name;
}
class FruitBox<T extends Fruit>
{
  private T box;
  public void FruitBox(T t) { box = t; }
  public String getFruitName()
  {
    // Use of Fruit member allowed since T extends Fruit
    return box.name;
  }
}
```

Generics and Object

Before generics were introduced in Java 5, the Object type was used to create container classes that could store any type of objects. Now that generics are available, this use of the Object type as a universal container should be avoided. That's because the compiler helps ensure that generics are type safe at compile-time, which can't be done when using the Object type.

The collection classes in the Java library, among them ArrayList, have all been replaced with generic versions. Even so, any generic class can still be used as if it weren't generic, simply by leaving out the type argument section. The default Object type will then be used as the type argument. That's why the non-generic version of ArrayList is still allowed. Consider the following use of a non-generic ArrayList:

```
import java.util.ArrayList;
// ...
// Object ArrayList
ArrayList a = new ArrayList();
a.add("Hello World");
// ...
Integer b = (Integer)a.get(0); // run-time error
```

This String-to-Integer conversion will fail at runtime by throwing a ClassCastException. Had a generic ArrayList been used instead, the mistaken conversion would have been detected upon compilation, or immediately in an IDE such as Netbeans. This compile-time debugging feature is a major advantage with using generics over other coding approaches:

```
import java.util.ArrayList;
// ...
// Generic ArrayList (recommended)
ArrayList<String> a = new ArrayList<String>();
a.add("Hello World");
// ...
Integer b = (Integer)a.get(0); // compile-time error
```

With the generic alternative, only the specified type argument will be allowed into the ArrayList collection. Additionally, values obtained from the collection don't have to be cast to the correct type because the compiler takes care of that.

CHAPTER 23

Lambda Expressions

Java 8 introduced the *lambda expression*, which provides a concise way to represent a method using an expression. A lambda expression consists of three parts: an argument list, the arrow operator (->), and a body. The following lambda takes two integer arguments and returns their sum:

```
(int x, int y) -> { return x + y; };
```

The parameter types generally don't need to be specified because the compiler can determine these types automatically. This type inference also applies to the return type. If the body contains only a single statement, you can leave out the curly brackets, and the result of the statement will then be returned:

```
(x, y) -> x + y;
```

Lambda objects

A lambda expression is a representation of a *functional interface*, which is an interface defining a single abstract method. It can therefore be bound to an object of such an interface provided that its functional method has a matching signature:

```
interface Summable
{
  public int combine(int a, int b);
}
```

© Mikael Olsson 2018
M. Olsson, *Java Quick Syntax Reference*, https://doi.org/10.1007/978-1-4842-3441-9_23

```
public class MyApp
{
  public static void main(String[] args) {
    Summable s = (x, y) -> x + y;
    s.combine(2, 3); // 5
  }
}
```

Common functional interfaces are defined in the java.util.function package added in Java 8. In this example, the BinaryOperator<T> interface can be used. It represents a method that takes two arguments and returns a result of the same type as the arguments. Its functional method is named apply:

```
import java.util.function.*;
public class MyApp
{
  public static void main(String[] args) {
    BinaryOperator<Integer> adder = (x, y) -> x + y;
    adder.apply(2, 3); // 5
  }
}
```

When working on a single operand and returning a value of the same type, you can use the UnaryOperator functional interface. Note that the parentheses surrounding the parameters can be left out when there's only one parameter:

```
UnaryOperator<Integer> doubler = x -> x*2;
doubler.apply(2); // 4
```

Lambda parameters

Unlike methods, lambda expressions don't belong to any class. They're objects in and of themselves as they're instances of functional interfaces. A benefit of this is that they provide a convenient way to pass functionality as an argument to another method. In the following example, the Runnable interface is used, which has a functional method that takes no parameters and returns no value. This interface belongs to java.lang, and its abstract method is named run:

```java
public class MyApp
{
  static void starter(Runnable s) { s.run(); }

  public static void main(String[] args) {
    Runnable r = () -> System.out.println("Hello");
    starter(r); // "Hello"
  }
}
```

You can also achieve this functionality by defining an anonymous (unnamed) inner class, but this approach is considerably more verbose than the lambda expression:

```java
Runnable r = new Runnable() {
  @Override public void run() {
    System.out.println("Hello");
  }
};
starter(r); // "Hello"
```

A lambda expression can capture variables from its context, provided that the referenced variable is final or effectively final (only assigned once). In this next example, the Consumer functional interface is used, which represents a function that accepts one parameter and returns no value:

```
import java.util.function.*;
public class MyApp
{
  final static String GREETING = "Hi ";

  public static void main(String[] args) {
    Consumer<String> c = (s) ->
      System.out.println(GREETING + s);
    c.accept("John"); // "Hi John"
  }
}
```

Behind the scenes, the compiler will instantiate an anonymous class containing a single method to represent a lambda expression. That enables lambdas to be fully backward-compatible with earlier versions of the Java runtime environment.

Index

A

Abstract class
    definition, 81
    and interfaces, 82–83
    Rectangle, 81–82
Access levels
    guideline, 67
    nested class, 66
    package-private, 64
    private, 63
    protected, 65
    public, 65
    top-level, 66
Anonymous code
    block, 11
ArithmeticException, 94
Arithmetic operators, 13
ArrayList class, 25
Arrays
    allocation, 23
    ArrayList class, 25
    assignment, 24
    declaration, 23
    definition, 23
    multi-dimensional, 24
Assignment operators, 14
Autoboxing, 96
Autounboxing, 96

B

Bitwise operators, 16
Boolean type, 10
Boxing and unboxing
    autoboxing and
        autounboxing, 96
    Integer object, 95
    primitive types, 95–96
    wrapper classes, 95–96
Break and continue statement, 33–34

C

Calling methods, 36
Catch block, 90
Char data type, 10
Checked and unchecked
    exceptions, 93
Class
    accessing object members, 42
    constructor (*see* Constructor)
    default values, 46
    definition, 41
    garbage collector, 47
    interface, 76
    null, 46
    object creation, 41–42
Code hints, 4

Get the eBook for only $5!

Why limit yourself?

With most of our titles available in both PDF and ePUB format, you can access your content wherever and however you wish—on your PC, phone, tablet, or reader.

Since you've purchased this print book, we are happy to offer you the eBook for just $5.

To learn more, go to http://www.apress.com/companion or contact support@apress.com.

Apress®

CPSIA information can be obtained
at www.ICGtesting.com
Printed in the USA
LVOW13s0815180518

577420LV00025B/99/P